Anger

CAUSES & EFFECTS OF EMOTIONS

CAUSES & EFFECTS
OF EMOTIONS

Anger

Rosa Waters

Mason Crest

Mason Crest
450 Parkway Drive, Suite D
Broomall, PA 19008
www.masoncrest.com

Printed and bound in the United States of America.

First printing
9 8 7 6 5 4 3 2 1

Series ISBN: 978-1-4222-3067-1
ISBN: 978-1-4222-3068-8
ebook ISBN: 978-1-4222-8761-3

The Library of Congress has cataloged the
hardcopy format(s) as follows:
          Library of Congress Cataloging-in-Publication Data

Waters, Rosa, 1957-
  Anger / Rosa Waters.
       pages cm. — (Causes & effects of emotions)
  Audience: Grade 7 to 8.
  Includes index.
  ISBN 978-1-4222-3068-8 (hardback) — ISBN 978-1-4222-3067-1 (series)
— ISBN 978-1-4222-8761-3 (ebook) 1. Anger—Juvenile literature. I. Title.
  BF575.A5W38 2014
  152.4'7—dc23
                                        2014004378

CONTENTS

KEY ICONS TO LOOK FOR:

 Text-Dependent Questions: These questions send the reader back to the text for more careful attention to the evidence presented there.

 Words to Understand: These words with their easy-to-understand definitions will increase the reader's understanding of the text, while building vocabulary skills.

 Series Glossary of Key Terms: This back-of-the book glossary contains terminology used throughout this series. Words found here increase the reader's ability to read and comprehend higher-level books and articles in this field.

 Research Projects: Readers are pointed toward areas of further inquiry connected to each chapter. Suggestions are provided for projects that encourage deeper research and analysis.

 Sidebars: This boxed material within the main text allows readers to build knowledge, gain insights, explore possibilities, and broaden their perspectives by weaving together additional information to provide realistic and holistic perspectives.

INTRODUCTION

The journey of self-discovery for young adults can be a passage that includes times of introspection as well joyful experiences. It can also be a complicated route filled with confusing road signs and hazards along the way. The choices teens make will have lifelong impacts. From early romantic relationships to complex feelings of anxiousness, loneliness, and compassion, this series of books is designed specifically for young adults, tackling many of the challenges facing them as they navigate the social and emotional world around and within them. Each chapter explores the social emotional pitfalls and triumphs of young adults, using stories in which readers will see themselves reflected.

Adolescents encounter compound issues today in home, school, and community. Many young adults may feel ill equipped to identify and manage the broad range of emotions they experience as their minds and bodies change and grow. They face many adult problems without the knowledge and tools needed to find satisfactory solutions. Where do they fit in? Why are they afraid? Do others feel as lonely and lost as they do? How do they handle the emotions that can engulf them when a friend betrays them or they fail to make the grade? These are all important questions that young adults may face. Young adults need guidance to pilot their way through changing feelings that are influenced by peers, family relationships, and an ever-changing world. They need to know that they share common strengths and pressures with their peers. Realizing they are not alone with their questions can help them develop important attributes of resilience and hope.

The books in this series skillfully capture young people's everyday, real-life emotional journeys and provides practical and meaningful information that can offer hope to all who read them.

It covers topics that teens may be hesitant to discuss with others, giving them a context for their own feelings and relationships. It is an essential tool to help young adults understand themselves and their place in the world around them—and a valuable asset for teachers and counselors working to help young people become healthy, confident, and compassionate members of our society.

Cindy Croft, M.A.Ed
Director of the Center for Inclusive Child Care at Concordia University

Words to Understand

evolved: Developed over a long period of time.

instinct: An automatic urge to act, without thinking about it.

aggressive: Fierce or ready for violence.

mobilizes: Gets ready to do something.

integrity: The quality of being ethical, or the state of being whole.

motivate: Encourage to do something.

Western: Having to do with European and American culture and society.

suppress: Push back; put an end to.

ONE

WHAT IS ANGER?

Imagine you're walking down the street, wearing your best clothes because you're headed for a job interview. A truck roars by, swerving through a puddle just as it goes past you—and now your clean, dressy clothes are soaked with muddy water. How do you feel?

Or say you tell your best friend something in confidence—and then you find out she's told your private information to everyone else in your group of friends. How do you feel?

What about if you're planning to go to a concert with your friends—but your parents say you can't go because you have to stay home and clean your very messy bedroom instead. How do you feel then?

If you're like most people, you feel angry in all these situations. Anger is an emotional response to something that threatens

Our emotions can function like caution signs, warning us to pay attention and be careful.

our well-being in some way. Something could endanger our well-being in a very small way or in an enormous way; it could threaten our physical health, our happiness, or our social standing. In all these cases, the emotion that's triggered is usually anger.

WHAT ARE EMOTIONS— AND WHY DO WE HAVE THEM?

We take our emotions—our internal feelings—for granted. They seem very *real* to us. But what are they really?

Scientists tell us that what we perceive as emotions are really changes in our bodies, especially changes in our brains. Different kinds of events trigger different responses inside us, and we've learned to give those responses labels—like "happiness," "love," "anger," and "fear."

Human beings' emotions do important jobs. They direct our attention toward things that are important. When something makes us happy, for example, our emotions say, "Notice this! Try to get more of this in your life!" Or when something scares us, our emotions tell us, "Be careful!" Our emotions act as bridges between the outside world, our inner responses, and the actions we need to take. We learn from our emotions; we learn what makes us happy and what makes us sad, what scares us and what makes us angry—and then we adjust our behavior accordingly. Positive emotions, like joy and excitement, inspire us to be creative and do amazing things—but negative feelings, like grief and boredom, can also serve important functions in our lives. Grief can make our bodies and minds shut down for a while, giving us a chance to recover from a loss, while boredom can spur us to change our lives, seeking out new challenges instead of being content to do the same thing over and over. Scientists believe we **evolved** with emotions because these internal reactions helped human beings cope better with external challenges. In other words, emotions helped us survive. Anger is no exception.

A SECONDARY EMOTION

Psychologists say that anger is a "secondary emotion." By that, they mean we usually have a primary reaction that comes first, before anger. So when that truck splashed you, maybe what you felt first was fear, because you were scared that when you got to the interview, you wouldn't get the job, thanks to the mud all over your clothes. When your friend revealed your private information to your other friends, you may have been hurt or embarrassed first, before you got angry. And when your parents wouldn't let you go to the concert, your initial response was probably disappointment.

But many times, anger is the first emotion of which we're aware. The primary emotion—fear, hurt, disappointment—is hidden beneath the anger. Unless we take time to step back and think about our reactions, we may never be aware of the primary emotion at all.

ANGER

What we interpret as an animal's anger may be only the fight-or-flight response.

FIGHT OR FLIGHT

Scientists believe that anger is actually a variation of the human fight-or-flight response. When humans—and all other animals as well—run into something that could be a threat to them, their bodies respond by getting them ready for whatever comes next. A whole bunch of physical reactions happen, like the heart beating faster and the muscles tensing, all of which are designed to give the body what it needs for an extra burst of energy to either fight or run away.

Fearful emotions are closely related to the fight-or-flight **instinct**, but so is anger. Anger is connected to the "fight" part of this response. When a person feels angry, chemicals well up in her brain that are designed to get her ready to take **aggressive** action. These chemicals evolved as a way to help animals drive away rivals for mates, be the first to get to the food, and scare

Make Connections: Do Animals Get Angry?

We often say that animals are angry. We talk about "angry bulls," "angry dogs," and even "angry bees." It's easy to think that animals get angry. Say you step on your cat's tail; when she arches her back and hisses at you, she looks angry. As humans, we've learned to label those kinds of reactions as "anger"—but animals don't have the ability to think about their feelings the same way we do. When we get angry, there's another element in our reaction besides just the perception of danger to our well-being. We blame the truck driver who splashed us, our friend who told our secrets, or our parents who wouldn't let us go to a concert. We believe they had a choice to act differently from what they did, and we think they were wrong to do what they did. Scientists don't believe animals are capable of attributing guilt like this. What they're feeling is really just fear. However, anger in humans and fear in animals do similar things within the body.

We experience anger in situations where we feel that other people—like our parents—aren't treating us fairly.

away other animals that might cause them harm. Anger serves pretty much the same purpose in our lives today. It **mobilizes** us to take action to get what we want.

Anger is a social emotion. In other words, we feel angry in situations where we see ourselves as being in a relationship with others, others whom we expect to behave in certain ways. We get angry when we think people aren't behaving the way they should within that relationship. When people treat us unfairly, when we don't feel like they're listening to us, when they tread on our toes in some way, when they don't treat us the way we feel we deserve to be treated, we get angry.

IS ANGER GOOD—OR BAD?

The answer to that question is: neither! Anger is just a feeling. It's a completely normal reaction to any situation that looks like a threat to you in some way. Feeling angry doesn't make you a bad person.

In fact, anger can give you the energy to do good things in the world. It's a signal that something is wrong. It tells you to pay attention—and then take action. In *The Dance of Anger*, psychologist Harriet Lerner writes:

> Anger is a signal and one worth listening to. Our anger may be a message that we are being hurt, that our rights are being violated, that our needs or wants are not being adequately met, or simply that something isn't right. Our anger may tell us that we are not addressing an important emotional issue in our lives, or that too much of our self—our beliefs, values, desires or ambitions—is being compromised in a relationship. . . . Just as physical pain tells us to take our hand off the hot stove, the pain of our anger preserves the very **integrity** of our self. Our anger can **motivate** us to say no to the ways in which we are defined by others and "yes" to the dictates of our inner self.

Angry women are often perceived differently from angry men. We use words like "hysterical," "witchy," and worse to describe women who are angry. People may make jokes, blaming women's anger on their menstrual cycles

Some psychologists suggest that we should think of anger as being like a smoke detector in a house or a warning light on a car dashboard. It's an indicator that something could be wrong, that we may need to take action.

It's what happens next, after we get angry, that's important. How we choose to express our anger can have either positive or negative consequences. For instance, during the Civil Rights Movement of the 1960s, people were angry that blacks were not treated the same as white people were—so people took action and changed America's laws to protect blacks' rights. That's an example of anger bringing about something positive. But suppose you and your friends were angry because you felt the school's grading policy was unfair; you decided to break all the windows in the school building and spray paint obscenities on the princi-pal's house. In this case, your anger led to violence. How you

Make Connections: Going Mad

The word "mad" originally had to do with violent excitement. It described a state where the person was so upset that he was "out of his mind." In other words, he was acting crazy; his mind was no longer controlling his behavior but instead his strong emotions were ruling him. Today, in the United States, if someone says, "I'm mad," she usually means, "I'm angry," and not "I'm crazy." But anger can also make a person act crazy!

chose to handle your anger was negative, rather than positive. We need to be able to respond to anger in positive and healthy ways. If we don't, it can get us in trouble.

MANAGING ANGER

Anger says to us, "Pay attention!" Once anger has gotten our attention, then we have an opportunity to take positive action. But here's the problem: if our anger continues to grow, we may lose our ability to think clearly about the situation. Anger revs up our

Make Connections: Women and Anger

In many cultures, anger is acceptable as a masculine emotion but it's considered inappropriate for women. Of course, women get angry just as much as men do, but they often learn to hide their anger. Sometimes they do such a good job, they don't even recognize it in themselves. It may come out at others indirectly, though (through behaviors like gossiping or complaining, for example), or it may lead to depression and poor self-images in women.

Research Project

In this chapter, you read that anger is often considered a more acceptable emotion for men than for women. Do you think this is true? Go online and see if you can find a recent news story about a woman politician or businessperson who got angry. What tone does the new article have? Do you think it would have had a different tone if the person who got angry were a man?

muscles and various body parts that will be needed for action—but in the process, it shuts down our brains. Researchers have found that anger decreases our ability to take in new information and come up with new ideas.

We're often told to express our feelings rather than bottling them up—but when it comes to managing our anger, psychologists have found that expressing it isn't always such a good idea. It all depends on how we express it. Venting our anger—either with words or actions—doesn't usually make us feel calmer or more clearheaded. Instead, it almost always makes us feel even angrier than we did before. Anger tends to feed on itself. It's like a snowball rolling downhill, getting bigger and faster the more it rolls. If we express our anger with aggression—either verbal or physical—we'll probably make the situation even worse. The other person will respond with her own anger. If she in turn takes action against us, now we have a new reason to be angry about, so we may do something even worse to the person who hurt us. The situation gets worse and worse. In fact, that's often how wars start!

Because anger is such a powerful emotion, people may feel uncomfortable with it. **Western** society has created certain taboos

Text-Dependent Questions

1. What is anger an emotional response to?
2. What is a secondary emotion?
3. What is the fight-or-flight response? Which part of this response is anger?
4. How is the way we feel anger different from what an animal might feel?
5. Why is venting our anger sometimes not a good idea?

about expressing anger, and we're taught these from the time we're very young children. Were you ever sent to time-out when you were little because you got mad and stomped your feet or shouted? Most of us learned that getting angry was "naughty." But the right response is not to **suppress** anger. When we bottle up our anger, it doesn't just go away. It's a better idea to learn to manage anger positively.

You want to be able to control your anger rather than letting it control you. The more you understand anger, the more you can use it as a positive force rather than a negative one.

Words to Understand

constrict: Squeeze or get smaller.
chronic: Lasting a long time.

TWO

WHAT HAPPENS TO YOU WHEN YOU FEEL ANGRY?

You've probably seen pictures of comic book characters with steam coming out of their ears. Or you may have heard people express anger with phrases like these: "I saw red," "It made my blood boil," or "I felt like I was going to explode." These images and sayings tell us that feeling angry has a physical side.

YOUR BODY'S REACTION TO ANGER

Physical responses to anger may vary from person to person. They can include clenching your teeth, frowning, flushing, and sweating. But no matter what you do on the outside—whether you yell

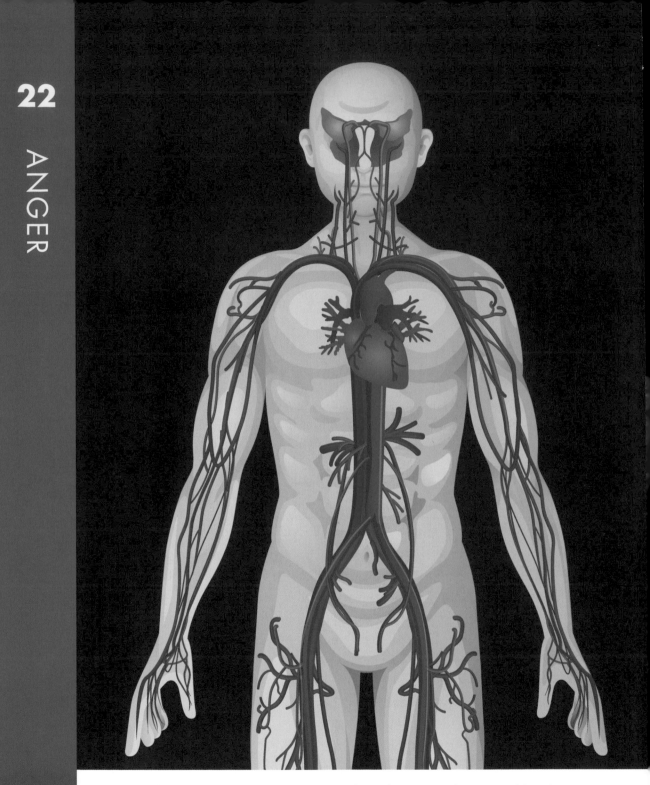

Fight-or-flight reactions make your heart beat faster, sending more blood through your blood vessels, to get your body ready to either fight or run away.

Make Connections: Different Expressions of Anger

 The experience of anger varies from person to person. Some people may cry when they feel angry, while someone else may yell, while still others may just get quiet when they're mad. This is partly because we all learned how to deal with anger from the families where we grew up. Some families do a lot of yelling and others don't. We tend to absorb all this as we're growing up. How our parents handled anger becomes a part of how we handle it too.

or say nothing, whether you stomp your feet or just quietly clench your fists—chemicals like adrenaline and noradrenaline are flooding through your body. These chemicals are what tell your body to get ready for fight-or-flight. Your body's preparations include these reactions:

- Heart rate and blood pressure increase.
- The pupils get bigger to take in as much light as possible
- The veins in the skin **constrict** to send more blood to major muscle groups.
- The amount of glucose (sugar) in the blood increases.
- Body muscles tense up, energized by adrenaline and glucose.
- The smooth muscles in other body organs relax in order to allow more oxygen into the lungs.
- Nonessential systems (like digestion and the immune system) shut down to allow more energy for emergency functions.
- The person has trouble focusing on small tasks, because the brain is directed to focus only on the big picture.

ANGER

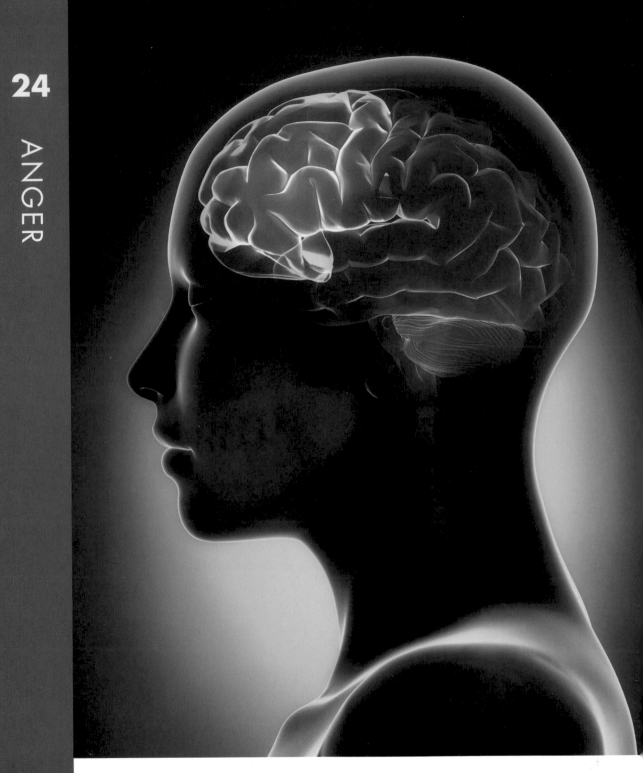

Your frontal lobe is the part of your brain that thinks things through.

Make Connections: Count to Ten!

Researchers have found that your amygdala's super-charged response lasts less than two seconds. That's why it's a good idea to count to ten when you're angry before you say or do anything. It gives your amygdala a chance to calm down, so that your more reasonable frontal lobe can take over.

Inside your brain, the amygdalae, the parts of the brain that deal with emotion, are going crazy. They're like a boxer jumping up and down, dancing in place, just waiting for the chance to throw the first punch. The amygdalae are eager to tell the rest of your body what action to take. They're the parts of your brain that wants you to slug someone or hurl a rock through a window.

Luckily, at the same time, something else is going on as well: blood flow is increasing to your frontal lobe, the part of your body that controls reasoning. Hopefully, your frontal lobe will be able to control your amygdalae long enough for them to calm down!

All these physical reactions to anger are normal and healthy. They're designed to protect you from threats, remember. The problem is, however, that most of the time in the modern world, the things that make us angry aren't people who are actually trying to kill us or take away our food. So the body's reactions that were meant to help us out can actually hurt us.

ANGER'S DESTRUCTIVE SIDE

Mark Twain—the same guy who wrote *Tom Sawyer* and *Huckleberry Finn*—once said, "Anger is an acid that can do more harm to the vessel in which it is stored than to anything on which it is poured." In other words, anger hurts you more than it hurts those

Research Project

Look online or in the library for more information about chronic anger. What are some signs that a person might be chronically angry? Look for more information about the health risks of chronic anger. How do the statistics compare to the health risks of smoking or heavy drinking?

around you. Mark Twain was right. If your anger reaction is constantly being triggered, it takes a toll on your body.

Think about it. If you're angry a lot, your heart is constantly being asked to beat harder. Your blood pressure will be higher much of the time. You're more likely to have a stroke. Eventually, your heart will start to wear out from all that extra stress. Studies have found that people who are angry much of the time have twice the risk of coronary disease and three times the risk of a heart attack, compared to people who have low levels of anger. High levels of anger also weaken your immune system, which means you may be more likely to catch colds, the flu, and other sicknesses. The message sent to your muscles to tense for fight will eventually mean you have lots of aches and pains and headaches. You may get stomachaches, which could eventually develop into

Make Connections: A Korean Proverb

If you kick a stone in anger,
you will hurt your foot.

Text-Dependent Questions

1. What are the two chemicals your body is flooded with during fight-or-flight?
2. What are three parts of your body's fight-or-fight response?
3. What do your amygdalae do? What about your frontal lobe?
4. What happens to your body if you're angry a lot?

serious conditions like ulcers. Scientists think that **chronic** anger may be even more dangerous to people's health than smoking and obesity.

Anger is a powerful emotion. It affects you on the inside, within your body—and it can also affect your outer life. Anger can either help or damage your relationships. It can give you the energy to overcome the challenges you face in life—or it can get in your way, keeping you from succeeding in life.

Words to Understand

destructive: Destroying or hurting someone or something.
passive: Accepting or allowing what others do.
snide: Rude or mocking.
constructive: Helping or building up others.
vulnerable: Open to being hurt.
retaliate: Make an attack in return for being previously hurt.
meditation: The practice of thinking deeply or focusing your mind for a
   period of time.

THREE

How Does Anger
Affect Your Life?

Has anyone ever said to you, "Getting angry won't solve anything"? The implied message, of course, is: "Don't get mad." While it's true that just being angry won't fix the problem—and venting your anger in negative ways could even make the problem worse—expressing your anger in the right way could lead to solving the problem.

ANGER STYLES

Psychologists have noticed that people generally express anger in one of three ways:

- Some people turn their anger outward in **destructive** ways. Psychologists sometimes refer to this as an aggressive style

If you're the sort of person who gets quiet and sulky when you're angry, you have a passive anger style that could end up making you feel sad and depressed.

of anger. It could include insulting people, swearing, throwing things or damaging property, and physically assaulting people.

- Some people turn their anger inward. This is also called a *passive* style of anger. It can often lead to depression. This can also become what psychologists refer to as "passive-aggressive" anger; people act passive on the outside, but their aggression leaks out in sneaky ways, such as sulking or being sarcastic and *snide*.

- Some people practice anger control, dealing with their anger in appropriate, positive, and *constructive* ways.

People may have a particular anger style that they mostly use, but a lot of people shift their styles, depending on the setting and circumstances. So, for example, you might act one way with your friends and a different way with your family, or one way with men and another way with women. Often people who use passive or passive-aggressive anger styles feel as though they're in a *vulnerable* position where the other person has the power to hurt them if they express their anger openly.

ANGER STYLES AND YOUR LIFE

Whether your anger style is aggressive, passive, or a combination of the two, anger has the power to hurt your relationships. It can come between you and the people you care about the most. It can turn your friends into your enemies, and it can make your family relationships painful. When your anger gets in the way, teachers or employers may not be able to see your real skills. All they see is your anger.

Moreover, because anger interferes with your ability to process information, anger that's not controlled can prevent you from completing tasks at school or on a job. When you're angry, it's harder to listen and harder to learn new things, so anger can hinder your school and work performance.

Think again about that truck that drove by and splashed you. You're standing on the sidewalk staring after the truck, and your heart is pounding. You feel hot all over. Now imagine that you react with an aggressive anger style. You do the first thing that pops into your head: you reach down, pick up a stone, and heave it at the back of the truck. You miss the truck altogether, but the stone hits a car that's coming toward you and smashes the windshield. The car pulls to a stop . . . and just then a police car you hadn't

Make Connections: The "Right" Way to Express Anger

When you express anger, psychologists suggest your goal should be to correct wrongdoing while maintaining your relationship with the person who has made you angry. This means that you want to defend your rights while still showing respect for the other person.

You may feel angry when your mom gives you a hard time about your clothes—but how you choose to handle that anger will shape the outcome of your argument.

noticed turns on its flashers and pulls over as well. Now you're in really big trouble! No matter what happens next, odds are good you're not going to make it to your job interview on time. Your aggressive anger style made the entire situation far worse than just having some mud on your clothes.

Next go back to the situation where your friend reveals your confidences to your entire group. You're sitting with your friends in the cafeteria, and they start laughing and talking about the secret you shared with your best friend. This time, imagine that you respond with a passive anger style. Your face is hot, your eyes are burning, and you've lost your appetite—but you don't say anything. Instead, you duck your head and stare at your tray until lunch is over. You avoid your friends for the rest of the day. Later, when you see your best friend's number come up on your cell phone, you ignore her call. By the time you go to bed, you realize you no longer feel angry. Now you just feel depressed. You lie in the dark and start to cry. "I hate myself," you whisper. Instead of attacking your friends, you're attacking yourself. And if you keep doing that, eventually you may pull away from your friends altogether. Because you no longer feel like you can trust your best friend, you stop hanging out with her. You start sitting alone during lunch. As the months go by, you turn into a loner, a person who has very few close relationships. Your passive anger style turned your anger inward—but your outside life ended up being damaged as well.

Now think about the concert your parents wouldn't let you go to because you had to clean your messy room. As soon as they tell you that you can't go, you're furious. You want to yell at them. You want to go to your room and slam your door. Instead, you take a deep breath. You wait a few seconds until you feel like you can think clearly. Finally, you say, "Can we at least talk about it? Could I clean my room another time? This concert is really important to me." You keep your voice calm. You listen to your parents' response. When they don't understand your position, you try again, still keeping your voice quiet. In the end, maybe they

Thinking again and again about the thing that made you mad may just make you stuck. You need to move on!

change their minds and let you go; maybe they don't. Either way, they respect you for handling the situation so maturely. They're impressed that you seem like you're growing up. They consider giving you more responsibilities and freedoms. You end up feeling closer to your parents than you did before.

COPING WITH ANGER

Knowing that we *should* control our anger isn't the same thing as being able to do it, though! Even if we make a habit of talking to our friends and family about our anger in a calm, respectful way, there are plenty of situations in life where that sort of self-expression just isn't possible. When that truck drove by and splashed you with muddy water, you couldn't chase after it and demand that the driver get out and listen while you expressed your feelings! In other cases, the thing that's making you angry may be too big or too far away for you to express yourself to it. For example, say you were turned down for a college scholarship; you may be angry at the organization that turned you down, but you can't talk directly to the people who made the decision. Or maybe you find out that someone you love has cancer, and you feel angry—but who are you angry *with*? God? Life? You may get some comfort by expressing your feelings through prayer—but you may also feel like there's no one to really hear your anger in a situation like this.

One of the worst things you can do is brood over your anger, going over and over it in your mind. We've all done that. Someone offended us during the day, and that night as we lie in bed, we find ourselves thinking about the insult again and again and again. It's as though we're hitting the instant-replay button over and over. Psychologists sometimes call this rumination. "Rumination" is what cows do with their cud, chewing and re-chewing the contents of their stomachs, so it's a good word for when you repeatedly relive an experience in your mind, replaying it, reviewing it, and reinterpreting it again and again.

Psychologists have found that when we ruminate on our anger—when we replay some incident that got us angry—we may

ANGER

Hopefully, you have more emotional options than this guy!

Make Connections: Lizard Brain?

Remember, when your anger gets the best of you, you're relying on your amygdala, which is the most primitive, least evolved part of the human brain. Some psychiatrists and neurologists refer to this as the "reptilian brain." This is because reptiles rely on a similar structure to control their instinctive behaviors, which include aggression, mating, catching prey, and dominating rivals. You don't really want to go through life functioning with the same skills a reptile has! Crocodiles, for example, aren't known for their ability to form strong bonds with other crocodiles, and you've probably never met a lizard that was warm and loving. You want to give your higher brain a chance to exercise its far more sophisticated skills, which will help you build and maintain the relationships that are important to you.

end up stuck, unable to get past our anger and move on. We may believe that by pondering the situation we're trying to gain understanding or get more information out of the situation. In fact, though, we're not really learning anything new. Instead, each time we go over the situation, we get angry all over again. When we're angry with someone, we feel that the other person is wrong and you're right. The more we think about it, the more reasons we come up with to justify our own positions—and the angrier we feel. Pretty soon, we end up chronically angry. We've got so much anger inside us that it spills out in situations where it's totally unjustified.

KICKING THE DOG

Say you've had a bad day at school. You got a D on a test, your girlfriend says she wants to break up, and the hall monitor yelled

Retaliation
Just Ahead

Retaliation isn't that much different from revenge. It's usually just quicker.

at you for no reason. As you trudge toward your house after school, you're going over in your mind everything that happened. When you trip over the family dog, it feels like the final straw. You give the dog a kick—and instantly feel guilty.

You're not really angry at the poor dog of course; you're really angry with your teacher, your girlfriend, and the hall monitor.

But you didn't let yourself express your anger to any of them. You didn't want to get in more trouble at school, and you didn't want to make your girlfriend even more upset with you. Instead, you just kept ruminating on your anger. Now your anger is coming out somewhere you won't get in trouble. Psychologists call it "displaced aggression." The more you ruminate on your anger, the more likely displaced aggression becomes.

OVERREACTING

Research led by psychologist Fred Bushman at the University of Michigan showed how likely people are to overreact to a minor annoyance after ruminating over a previous insult. In Bushman's study, people were interrupted and humiliated while doing a difficult task. Some people were then asked to think about the experience, and some were distracted from mulling it over. When all of them were later given a chance to get back at the research assistant who interrupted them, those who had been ruminating were much more likely to **retaliate**.

Psychologists say that ruminating on anger can also makes us more likely to perceive threats and insults around us. Imagine you're walking through the mall going over a fight you just had with your sister. By the time you reach the food court, you're seething. A woman who's talking on her cell phone doesn't see you (even though you're right in front of her) and bumps into you. If you were in a calmer frame of mind, you would assume she wasn't paying attention; you'd say, "Excuse me," and go on your way. But because your mind is churning with angry thoughts, you see her careless behavior as an affront to you. You jump to the conclusion that she ran into you on purpose. You snarl at her, "Watch where you're going!" An innocent mistake turns into an ugly scene.

STEPPING BACK

So what should you do? Research has found that exercise is a good way to get rid of some of the tension anger causes. So is

Research Project

Think of a time recently when you've become angry. How did you handle your anger? What type of anger style from chapter 2 is this? Using the techniques described in this chapter, write down how you could have handled your anger more constructively or coped with it better.

meditation. Doing anything you enjoy—whether that's reading a good book, watching your favorite TV show, listening to music, or playing a video game—can help your body relax and give your brain a chance to get some perspective on the situation. Think about something funny. It's almost impossible to laugh and be angry at the same time! Talking to someone also helps.

Make Connections: Catch Yourself!

Pay attention to how long you allow yourself to replay an infuriating scenario in your head. After about twenty minutes, the initial burst of anger—your body's physical responses to a threat—will usually wear off. If you're still thinking about the incident, that's a good sign that you're starting to ruminate. Catch yourself before you chew the cud of anger any longer. Break the cycle by distracting yourself. If you can think about something else for a while, when your thoughts do go back to the incident, it may not seem as bad.

Text-Dependent Questions

1. What are the three ways people express their anger?
2. What anger styles are you more likely to use if you feel vulnerable?
3. What are two ways aggressive and passive anger can hurt your life?
4. Why is brooding over your anger one of the worst things you can do?
5. What are two ways to deal with the tension anger causes?

But the way you talk is important. Psychologists have found that when people talk endlessly about situations that make them angry, they often end up even angrier than before. If when they talk, they constantly rehash the things that triggered their anger in the first place, it's the same thing that happens during rumination: their bodies react all over again.

When people can talk calmly, though, stepping back from the situation to gain some perspective, research shows that their blood pressure goes down. While they look for solutions, their bodies calm down too. Now that their brains can function again, they can begin to pay attention to what their anger is actually saying.

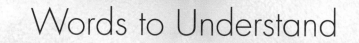

Words to Understand

paradoxical: Absurd or contradictory; having to do with two things that can't be true at the same time.
socially: Having to do with people's interactions.

FOUR

LEARNING
FROM ANGER

Remember the Incredible Hulk of comic book, television, and movie fame? Whenever mild-mannered Dr. Banner got angry, he would swell to enormous proportions (turning green in the process) and start breaking things. His anger was huge and destructive. It took over, wiping out all of Dr. Banner's otherwise gentle personality and intelligence. The Hulk was impressive—but he was also really stupid.

Something similar happens to all of us when we get angry. We don't turn green, and we don't swell so big that we rip the seams of our clothes—but we often do stupid things when we're angry that we never would do otherwise. Researchers tell us that anger makes us see only black and white, no shades of gray. When we're angry, we think, "I'm good—he's bad." We tell ourselves, "I'm *completely* right, and she's *completely* wrong." We're

Anger is like a stop sign. It means you should step back from the situation, take a look at what's actually happening, and then listen to the other person's perspective.

not willing to compromise. Our brains' problem-solving skills are swamped. Angry behavior isn't intelligent behavior!

But it doesn't have to be that way. We don't have to turn into the Hulk when we get angry. Instead, we can learn from our anger.

STOP, LOOK, AND LISTEN

A good way to learn from anger is to think of anger as a stop sign. If you're driving and you see a stop sign on the road, you don't stop your car, get out, grab the stop sign, and start hitting passersby with it. And you don't grab the sign and hit yourself over the head with it either. Stop signs tell you to stop, look, and listen before continuing on your way. Anger should do the same thing.

Psychiatrist Susan Heitler offers these recommendations:

STOP

Stop moving forward in the current interaction. Pause for a moment of silence so you can breathe deeply, and use whatever you have in your bag of tricks for lowering your emotional intensity (distraction, relaxation, count to ten, etc). Stop moving forward on the hot topic by pleasantly making a left turn onto another pathway: . . . "Excuse me. I need a drink of water," you might say as you stand up and walk into another room. Then distract yourself, breathe deeply, sit in your quieting chair, and when you are calmer plan how you will handle the situation more effectively when you return from your time-out.

LOOK

Look at the situation from a fresh perspective to figure out what you really want. Then think of an alternative strategy, a more clever way than bludgeoning your dialogue partner with anger, to get what you want. This is where you have a big advantage over bulls or lions.

When you're yelling at the other person, you're not giving yourself a chance to stop and look at what's really going on—and you're definitely not listening!

You can use *words* to analyze your situation, explain your concerns, and create a plan for what you might do differently.

Beware! There's a potential trap here. I call it the "locus of focus" trap. Your focus must be on yourself, not on the person at whom you feel angry. Stay clear of thoughts about what you want the *other* person to do differently. A focus on how to get the other person to do what you want will escalate your frustration and anger.

Your focus needs to be on yourself, that is, on what *you* yourself could do to handle the situation more effectively. Empowering yourself instead of controlling others is a key component of overcoming anger tendencies, so again and again remind yourself when you're getting mad, "My job is to figure out what I myself can do differently to get what I want, not to tell others what they should do."

LISTEN

Here's the hardest part. Ask about the other person's concerns, and then listen attentively for what makes sense to you about their answers. Listen to truly understand their perspective, not to tell them what's wrong with their viewpoint. When you are angry, genuinely listening to the person you are mad at can feel remarkably difficult. That's because of a perceptual shift that anger evokes *When you are angry, you will feel as if what you want is sacred, and what the other person wants is irrelevant.* Your wants will loom huge; others' will shrink to virtual nothingness.

You'll have to be sure therefore that you have thoroughly calmed yourself during your initial Stop. That's essential so that when you get to *Listen*, you will be able to hear others' concerns. Fortunately, if you truly do listen well enough to understand sympathetically the

A toolbox holds lots of different tools, each with its own use—and the more options you have in your anger "toolbox," the more likely you'll be to find one that works in each situation.

other person's perspective, you will have higher odds of getting what *you* want! Sound **paradoxical**? It is, and it is very real. Ask any skillful salesperson. The more a salesperson understands his customer's concerns, the more likely that they will reach an agreement.

That's because listening to truly understand the other person is critical to . . . collaborative problem-solving. . . . Win-win solution-building is far more effective than anger as a strategy for getting folks what they want. In addition, talking together cooperatively to find solutions that work for both of you keeps your relationships, at work and at home, strong and positive.

ANGER-MANAGEMENT TOOLS

You're going to get angry. Life is bound to frustrate you or disappoint you or hurt you—and when that happens, you're likely to respond with anger. There are tools you can use, though, to help you manage your anger.

These tools will vary, depending on the circumstances. In one situation, for example, you might want to go for a walk until you're calmer—but in another situation that won't be possible. That doesn't mean you can't still manage your anger; it just means you need to use different tools in different situations. The same way you might use a hammer to pound a nail, but reach for a pair of pliers if you need to turn a screw that's stuck, you can pick and choose your anger tools to fit the situation at hand. It's a good idea, though, to have as many tools as possible in your toolbox. That way no matter the circumstances, you'll have a tool handy that will work for that particular situation.

Here are few of the tools you'll want to have:

- Get in the habit of taking three deep breaths whenever you notice you're starting to feel angry. When you are angry, your body becomes tense. Breathing deeply will ease the tension and help lower your anger level.

Taking three deep breaths not only gives you a chance to stop and step back from the situation, but the extra oxygen will also help to calm your body's fight-or-flight response.

- When it's possible to do so, change your environment. The quickest way to disconnect yourself from a source of anger is to take a five-minute walk to get some fresh air.
- Know why you feel angry. Track down the primary emotions that lie under your anger. Anger often masks fears and hurts. If you can identify the emotion that's at the root of your anger, you may be able to move past the anger too.
- Make a habit of *responding* to the situation rather than *reacting* to it. Often, when you get angry, there's a situation that does require a response—but don't react by doing the first thing that pops into your head. Think about the scenario where the truck splashed you with muddy water. The situation required a response: you needed to figure out a way to get your clothes wiped off before you went to your interview. But if you reacted by throwing a stone at the truck, you did nothing to actually help the situation!
- Where it's appropriate and safe, respond to the situation by standing up for yourself. It's not okay to let people hurt you, either physically or emotionally. Set healthy limits and boundaries—and when others cross them, defend yourself respectfully but firmly. Be assertive but not aggressive.
- When it's possible, take time out to think before you respond. Before you speak out, be clear about what the real issue is, what you want to accomplish, and how to maximize the chances you will be heard.
- When you can't safely or appropriately confront the situation directly, avoid it. Don't put yourself in the position where you're going to encounter the same offense over and over.
- Take a step back from the situation. When you're in the grip of anger, your judgment is clouded and your perceptions are distorted. You want to give your higher brain a chance to kick in, while your more primitive amygdala calms down. Take a few deep breaths. Hum a few bars of your favorite song. Pray. Anything that allows you to step back from your body's automatic reactions will empower you.

Arguments come to a standstill when both sides refuse to talk. Be willing to be the first to break the silence.

- Instead of ruminating on your anger, focus on areas of your life where you feel in control. Think about the things you do well. Ruminate on all that's going right in your life.
- Develop your sense of humor. Laughter drives out anger.
- Get plenty of physical exercise. It's good for your body, and research shows that it helps you cope better with your emotions, including anger.
- Don't be afraid to try new things. Go outside your comfort zone to build on your existing strengths. The more things you know how to do, the more skills you will have to face life's challenges, and the less likely you are to feel frustrated and helpless, which can in turn trigger anger as a secondary emotion.
- Set realistic expectations for yourself and others. If, for example, you're getting angry with your boyfriend because he doesn't write you romantic poems, maybe you need to lower your expectations of him. He may not be the type of guy who will ever write a poem, and you're not being fair if you're expecting him to do something that's just not part of his personality.
- Pay attention to people's positive qualities. Your boyfriend who doesn't write you love poems may also be loyal, gentle, and kind. If you're so focused on your anger that he won't act exactly the way you want him to act, you may miss all the wonderful things he *does* do—and as you focus more on these positive things, you'll find you feel less angry with him.
- Be open to others' perspective. Don't expect others to only hear your point of view; be willing to listen to theirs as well.
- Don't take everything personally. When your mother snaps at you because you forgot to do your chores, she may not actually be angry with you; she may have something on her mind on which she's ruminating.
- Be willing to be the person who takes the first step toward making the situation better. If, instead, you hold on to your

Don't get mad at someone because he can't read your mind!

need to be right, while you wait for someone else to be willing to act, the situation may never change—and it may get worse, both for you and for everyone.

- Don't use "below-the-belt" tactics when talking to someone who has made you angry. These tactics include blaming, ordering, threatening, insulting, ridiculing, and lecturing.
- Get in the habit of using "I" language, both when speaking and thinking. Instead of saying, "You make me so angry," say, "I feel so angry when you. . ." This shifts the blame off the other person. Learn to take responsibility for your anger rather than putting that responsibility on others.
- Don't expect people to know what you want from them if you don't tell them. They're not mind readers!
- Don't make vague requests. For example, don't tell your best friend, "I want you to be nice to me." Let the other person know specifically what you want. ("I don't like it when you make fun of my clothes. Please don't do that anymore.")
- Don't get caught up in silly arguments that go nowhere. Don't waste your energy trying to convince someone that you're right. Instead, say something like, "Well, maybe it sounds crazy to you, but that's how I feel," or "I guess we see the problem differently." And then let it go.
- Don't expect people to change overnight—and don't expect yourself to change quickly either! When change comes, it comes slowly.
- Let go of what is beyond your control. You can only change yourself and your responses to others.
- Make positive statements to yourself. Memorize a few positive statements to think whenever your anger is triggered. These will help you remember that you can choose other ways to respond besides anger. You might say, "He has a right to his opinions," "She is doing the best she can," or "I am able to make good choices."

Learning to handle your anger doesn't mean you can't stand up for yourself—but you'll learn new, more effective ways to do that. Sometimes you can do more with a smile on your face than you can by yelling or pouting.

FORMING NEW HABITS

Like much of life, the way we handle anger is a habit. Habits are behaviors we do over and over without thinking. They're just part of our daily life, and many times we don't even think about them. We just do them, without giving them a thought one way or another. The good news is that we can get rid of old habits and form new ones.

Make Connections: Myths About Anger

Ignore it and it will go away.
Reality: Anger that's not addressed in some way, usually comes out in more harmful ways.

Time heals all wounds.
Reality: Time alone won't take care of anger. Rumination can even make anger get worse with time, like a wound that gets infected instead of healing.

Let it out and you'll feel better.
Reality: Blowing up may make you feel better at the time, but it actually can make you feel worse in the long run. Explosive bursts of anger are hard on your body—and they can damage relationships that are important to you.

If I'm not angry, others will walk all over me.
Reality: Anger frequently gets results in the short term, and therefore is an easy habit to develop. However, in the long term, it pushes people away and makes people less willing to respect you.

I can't help the way I act. I'm an angry person.
Reality: This attitude confuses feeling and acting. Because you feel a certain way does not mean you have to act that way.

Other people and situations are what make me angry.
Reality: Not everybody gets angry at the same things. We make ourselves angry by the way in which we interpret events. Don't give circumstances outside you the power to control your frame of mind!

In *The Power of Habit: Whey We Do What We Do in Life and Business*, Charles Duhigg explain how habits work and how we can change them. He writes:

> First, there is a cue, a trigger that tells your brain to go into automatic mode and which habit to use. Then there is the routine, which can be physical or mental or emotional. Finally, there is a reward, which helps your brain figure out if this particular loop is worth remembering for the future. Over time, this loop . . . becomes more and more automatic. The cue and reward become intertwined.

So when it comes to managing our habit, here's how you can form a new habit. Pay attention to the *cue*, the trigger that tells your brain to go into automatic mode. In this case, it's the feeling of anger. Then, instead of doing whatever you normally do when you feel angry, decide to try a new set of behaviors: stop, pay attention, and choose a tool from your anger "tool box." You may need to experiment a little. Figure out which tools work best for you—and then once you have, reach for those tools again and again.

Text-Dependent Questions

1. How is our anger similar to the Incredible Hulk's?
2. What is the "stop" part of Susan Heitler's recommendations? What are some ways to do it?
3. What is the "locus of focus" trap in the "look" part of Dr. Heitler's recommendations?
4. What is the hardest part of Dr. Heitler's recommendations? Why is it so difficult?
5. What are four of the anger-management tools given in this chapter?

The reward will come with the increased sense of well-being you'll feel, physically, emotionally, and **socially**. Pretty soon, if you stick with it, your brain will have built a new loop, an automatic cycle from cue to action to reward.

Anger can damage our bodies. It can hurt our relationships with others, and it can make us unhappy and miserable. But anger can also be a powerful source of energy that pushes us toward a happier life. It can empower you. So next time you feel angry, stop, pay attention, choose an anger management tool. Make it a habit!

Find Out More

IN BOOKS

Greenwald, Anna. *I'm Not Bad, I'm Just Mad: A Workbook to Help Kids Control Their Anger.* Oakland, CA: Instant Help, 2008.

Huebner, Dawn. *What to Do When Your Temper Flares: A Kid's Guide to Overcoming Problems With Anger.* Washington, DC: Magination Press, 2007.

Lohmann, Raychelle Cassada. *The Anger Workbook for Teens: Activities to Help You Deal with Anger and Frustration.* Oakland, CA: Instant Help, 2009.

ONLINE

Dealing with Anger: The Fire Inside
pbskids.org/itsmylife/emotions/anger

How Can I Deal with My Anger?
teenshealth.org/teen/your_mind/emotions/deal_with_anger.html

Taking Charge of Anger
kidshealth.org/kid/feeling/emotion/anger.html

Series Glossary of Key Terms

adrenaline: An important body chemical that helps prepare your body for danger. Too much adrenaline can also cause stress and anxiety.

amygdala: An almond-shaped area within the brain where the flight-or-flight response takes place.

autonomic nervous system: The part of your nervous system that works without your conscious control, regulating body functions such as heartbeat, breathing, and digestion.

cognitive: Having to do with thinking and conscious mental activities.

cortex: The area of your brain where rational thinking takes place.

dopamine: A brain chemical that gives pleasure as a reward for certain activities.

endorphins: Brain chemicals that create feelings of happiness.

fight-or-flight response: Your brain's reaction to danger, which sends out messages to the rest of the body, getting it ready to either run away or fight.

hippocampus: Part of the brain's limbic system that plays an important role in memory.

hypothalamus: The brain structure that gets messages out to your body's autonomic nervous system, preparing it to face danger.

limbic system: The part of the brain where emotions are processed.

neurons: Nerve cells found in the brain, spinal cord, and throughout the body.

neurotransmitters: Chemicals that carry messages across the tiny gaps between nerve cells.

serotonin: A neurotransmitter that plays a role in happiness and depression.

stress: This feeling that life is just too much to handle can be triggered by anything that poses a threat to our well-being, including emotions, external events, and physical illnesses.

Index

About the Author & Consultant

Rosa Waters lives in New York State. She has worked as a writer for several years, producing works on health, history, and other topics.

Cindy Croft is director of the Center for Inclusive Child Care at Concordia University, St. Paul, Minnesota where she also serves as faculty in the College of Education. She is field faculty at the University of Minnesota Center for Early Education and Development program and teaches for the Minnesota on-line Eager To Learn program. She has her M.A. in education with early childhood emphasis. She has authored *The Six Keys: Strategies for Promoting Children's Mental Health in Early Childhood Programs* and co-authored *Children and Challenging Behavior: Making Inclusion Work* with Deborah Hewitt. She has worked in the early childhood field for the past twenty years.

Picture Credits